365 Days of Drawing

This book belongs to:

Haley M. Fossgreen

Haley.fossgreen19@gmail.com
or
Haley-Fossgreen@istafrica.com

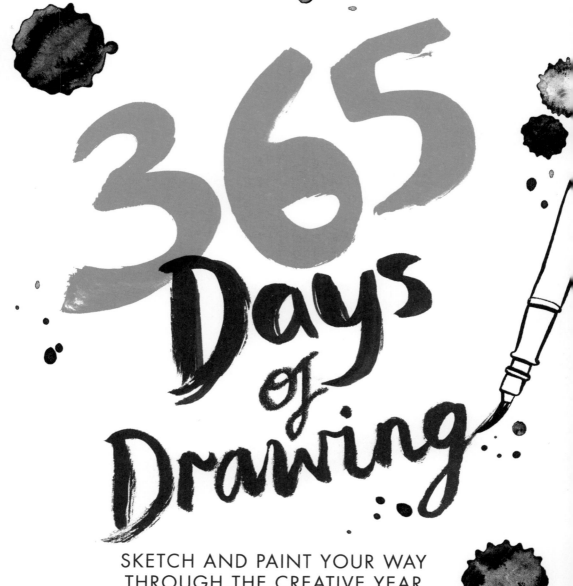

365 Days of Drawing

SKETCH AND PAINT YOUR WAY THROUGH THE CREATIVE YEAR

LORNA SCOBIE

Hardie Grant

BOOKS

Welcome to 365 Days of Drawing!

Whilst the notion of drawing may automatically evoke images of black-and-white tones, the term drawing has come to encompass a broader range of artistic styles, techniques and mediums, including those making use of colour. Whether you use a crayon to create simple expressive marks, or complete a detailed sketch of the human face, all drawing can provide a welcome break from our busy lives. I firmly believe that absolutely *everyone* can draw – and as with other skills, drawing can be learnt, practised and honed. We can draw in the sand with our hands, on a window pane with our finger, with pastels in colour and, in my opinion, even using paint.

Within this book there is a creative activity for you to complete every day of the year, however, you can do them in any way you like over any period of time, so that it best suits your lifestyle. Don't feel any pressure to complete all the tasks or approach them in any particular order. This is *your* book, and there isn't a right or wrong way of working. Just use the chart on the next page to tick off the activities as you go.

Each activity has been given a category. These include Imagination, Tutorial, Relaxation, Colour Theory and Observational and have all been colour-coded so that you can identify them inside the book. The categories help give you a broad approach to drawing, and over the course of the book, you can try out a range of different ways to draw and discover what you enjoy most. Every activity in this book encourages and nurtures your creativity, regardless of how simple or complex they may seem. Setting time aside every day to draw will help you improve your confidence, skill level and provide a little relaxation.

IMAGINATION Drawing doesn't have to be realistic, and the imagination tasks offer the chance to enjoy yourself without worrying about accuracy. A key part of drawing is allowing your mind to wander. Using your imagination is an integral part of being creative, so it's an excellent skill to practise.

TUTORIAL The guided tutorial activities introduce drawing techniques to help sharpen your skills. Explore sketching objects, investigate adding tone and practise drawing people – it is your chance to tackle a technique you find difficult or tend to avoid; or maybe you simply want to concentrate on a more structured activity that requires your full attention. It's a good idea to have a go at these tasks when you have a little more time available, in a calm setting where you can focus completely.

RELAXATION The relaxation tasks encourage you to be mindful whilst you draw. They require less focused thought than other tasks, and will provide a calming way for you to switch off from the busy world. They are perfect to do while listening to music or even on a long journey. Let yourself lose track of time and any other tasks on your mind and take pleasure in being in the moment. Explore colour, shape and pattern without feeling any pressure about what the finished drawing will be.

COLOUR THEORY In the colour theory activities you will be exploring the relationship between colours, how different hues can change the mood and feel of your drawing and which colours you personally enjoy working with. Applying colour to your drawings can feel overwhelming at times so these activities are designed to help simplify the challenge and to help you understand the way colour works.

OBSERVATIONAL The observational drawing activities will give you the opportunity to practise drawing from life. It is by learning to really *look*, and *see*, that enables us to improve our drawing skills. Sketching outside, whether it be people, buildings or nature, can be a useful way to practise observational drawing, and you may want to complete these activities out and about. I hope that these tasks encourage you to see *everything* with fresh eyes, as all the things around you become possible subjects for your drawings.

Although there is no end goal for your creativity, there is a chance at the end of the book to put your accumulated skills into practise. Completing a sustained drawing for each category will help to recap everything you've discovered about how you like to draw.

The most important thing to keep in mind is to enjoy the process. Use this book to add a little more creativity into your daily life and have fun! Don't worry about your drawing being 'good' or 'bad' as any form of creative mark making is a success. Just go for it. I hope that the tasks inspire you to continue drawing outside of the book, and that your own personal style develops over time. Whatever happens, I am optimistic that once completing your year of drawing, you will be more confident about your artistic abilities and feel excited by where this could lead you.

Your creations can be personal and private, but if you'd like to share them, do so with pride! Use the hashtag **#365DaysOfDrawing** to share your art with the online community.

Activities Completed

KEY: ■Imagination ■Tutorial ■Relaxation ■Colour theory ■Observational

1	2	3	4	5	6	7	8	9	10
11	12	13	14	15	16	17	18	19	20
21	22	23	24	25	26	27	28	29	30
31	32	33	34	35	36	37	38	39	40
41	42	43	44	45	46	47	48	49	50
51	52	53	54	55	56	57	58	59	60
61	62	63	64	65	66	67	68	69	70
71	72	73	74	75	76	77	78	79	80
81	82	83	84	85	86	87	88	89	90
91	92	93	94	95	96	97	98	99	100
101	102	103	104	105	106	107	108	109	110
111	112	113	114	115	116	117	118	119	120
121	122	123	124	125	126	127	128	129	130
131	132	133	134	135	136	137	138	139	140
141	142	143	144	145	146	147	148	149	150
151	152	153	154	155	156	157	158	159	160
161	162	163	164	165	166	167	168	169	170
171	172	173	174	175	176	177	178	179	180

181	182	183	184	185	186	187	188	189	190
191	192	193	194	195	196	197	198	199	200
201	202	203	204	205	206	207	208	209	210
211	212	213	214	215	216	217	218	219	220
221	222	223	224	225	226	227	228	229	230
231	232	233	234	235	236	237	238	239	240
241	242	243	244	245	246	247	248	249	250
251	252	253	254	255	256	257	258	259	260
261	262	263	264	265	266	267	268	269	270
271	272	273	274	275	276	277	278	279	280
281	282	283	284	285	286	287	288	289	290
291	292	293	294	295	296	297	298	299	300
301	302	303	304	305	306	307	308	309	310
311	312	313	314	315	316	317	318	319	320
321	322	323	324	325	326	327	328	329	330
331	332	333	334	335	336	337	338	339	340
341	342	343	344	345	346	347	348	349	350
351	352	353	354	355	356	357	358	359	360
361	362	363	364	365					

Materials

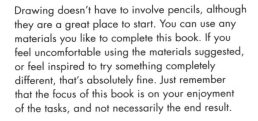

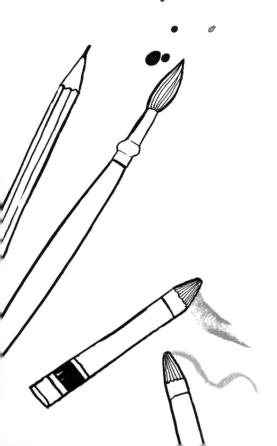

Drawing doesn't have to involve pencils, although they are a great place to start. You can use any materials you like to complete this book. If you feel uncomfortable using the materials suggested, or feel inspired to try something completely different, that's absolutely fine. Just remember that the focus of this book is on your enjoyment of the tasks, and not necessarily the end result.

Your materials don't need to be expensive. I have suggested a few of my favourite ones here, but these are by no means a necessity. I have seen artists creating the most incredible artwork with the humble blue biro (ballpoint), and if this is what you most enjoy using, use it! Within this book I do encourage you to use a range of different materials so that you can explore new techniques, and have fun expanding your collection over time.

Visit art shops for a large range of materials, and make use of the staff who can offer excellent advice about different pens, pencils and paints to suit your needs. Explore stationery shops which have a great variety of pens and pencils too and browse online for material recommendations. You could also swap tips with friends and discuss thoughts with fellow creatives on social media.

If you are concerned about the materials you use bleeding through the page (as some ink pens and paints might), you could prime the paper with clear gesso before you start your activity. This will form a layer between the paper and the material and will prevent bleeding – just be sure to allow plenty of time for the gesso to dry before you start.

Pencils

Pencils range in softness, most commonly from a 9B, which will create a very soft black line, to a 9H, which is very hard and creates a very sharp, light line. It might be useful to have a variety of pencils so you can experiment with the different effects they make. Try a 3B for shading and an H or 2H for crisp lines.

Mechanical pencils are also a great tool to have. Despite still containing a pencil lead, these feel more like a pen to hold, as they are metal or plastic and often have a rubber grip for your fingers. I enjoy using the Staedtler Mars Micro 0.5, and the Pentel P205 0.5. Mechanical pencils don't need sharpening, but you will need to buy extra refills for them. Make sure you choose the correct size of refill for your pencil. (The mechanical pencil will say the refill it takes on its side.)

If you are using pencils, you'll also need a good eraser and pencil sharpener.

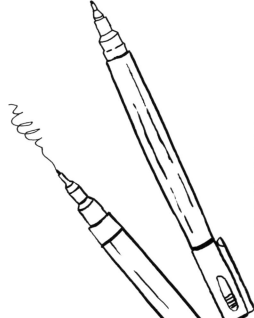

Fine liner pens

It's really useful to have a few black fine liner pens in your kit. These can be used for anything from jotting down notes and ideas, to quick sketches and adding details to artwork. There is a wide range of brands and nib sizes to choose from, so I recommend experimenting with the testers in an art store to see which you prefer. My favourites include the Uni Pin Fine Line pens, the Sakura Pigma Micron pens and the Derwent Graphik Line Maker pens, but there are plenty more to choose from.

Coloured pencils

Coloured pencils are a quick, easy and relatively mess-free. My favourite sets are the Staedtler Ergosoft pencils, which are hard and create a very solid, bright colour, and the Caran d'Ache Supracolor pencils, which have a softer lead and come in a huge range of colours. In art stores you can also buy individual coloured pencils, so you can choose the perfect colour and style. I really enjoy the hues available in the Faber-Castell Polychromos range. Some coloured pencils are water-soluble, so you can blend them with water and a paint brush to create colour blends.

I find it very handy to have some extra black pencils as I seem to go through these quickly. You could also try thicker black pencils like the Conte à Paris Pierre Noir HB, which has a charcoal feel to it.

Watercolour paints

Sizes of watercolour palettes can vary. It's convenient to have more colours in your palette, but the smaller sets are also great and you can mix colours to create a whole rainbow of hues. Daler Rowney and Winsor & Newton both produce wonderfully vibrant colours. When you run out of a particular colour, you can even purchase individual replacements so your set of watercolours can last forever!

Paint brushes vary greatly too, and it's useful to have a range of brush sizes and shapes. Tips can be pointed, rounded and even flat, and each will produce a different effect. Experiment with different types. You'll also need a container for your water, which can be anything from a mug to an empty yoghurt pot, and some paper towel for blotting water off your brush. Make sure your brush is wet before you use it to pick up watercolour paint, and rinse it in the water before changing colour to keep your colours clean. You could also try water brush pens. These brushes can be filled with water and provide a useful alternative way of painting with watercolours.

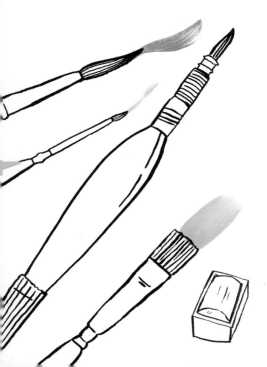

Most palettes come with a space inside the lid to mix the colours – a mixing palette. These can be revisited even when the paint has dried out, just by applying a bit of water from your brush. You can also buy additional mixing palettes if you prefer to have more space.

Wax Pastels

These are a really fun material to use as they slide easily over paper and you can cover large areas quickly when using them on their sides. There is a great range of colours which can be bought individually or in sets, and you can even buy grips to stop your hands getting too messy! I like the Caran d'Ache Neocolor II Aquarelle pastels which are water-soluble. Just add a little water to your wax pastel drawing using a brush or sponge for an interesting effect.

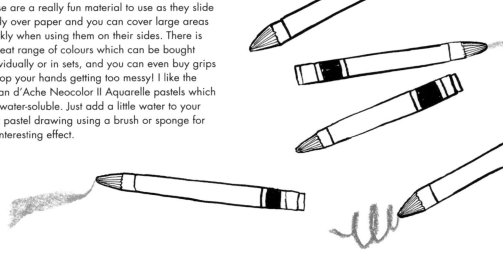

Here are some other materials you may like to have in your art kit:

- **Sketchbooks:** Use these to continue your creative journey. They are a great place to experiment and record your ideas, and come in a huge range of sizes.

- **Clear gesso:** A primer to apply with a clean brush to paper or board to prevent materials from bleeding.

- **Gouache:** These are water-based paints, similar to watercolour, but provide a more intense colour as they are more opaque. They dry quickly, but are great if you're interested in layering colours.

- **Scissors:** For collages and cutting paper.

- **Glue:** PVA or a gluestick can be used to stick down collages. Water down PVA to make it less gloopy.

- **Masking tape (sticky tape):** Handy for sticking down things quickly, and easy to remove and draw on.

- **Tracing paper:** Stick this over drawings which are a bit messy, using masking tape.

- **Charcoal:** A great material to explore tone. They can get messy.

- **Acrylic paint:** Strong, bright colours, which dry quickly and can also be watered down. Be sure to wash brushes before the paint on them dries.

- **Coloured paper:** This always comes in handy and you could collect it is as you go. You could even use gift wrap or brown paper bags. Origami paper is useful as it is thin, and easy to tear.

- **Brush tip pens:** These come in great colours and can be an excellent tool to draw with.

- **Bulldog clips:** Useful for holding back the rest of your pages whilst you work on an activity.

1. Begin by roughly drawing the shape of the object. If it is round, sketch a circle with roughly the correct shape. Then add more detail and accurate lines until you are happy with it.

2. Eventually, you are aiming to draw the outline straightaway, without roughly sketching a shape beforehand. Practise drawing the object until you can do this. Move your eye slowly around the edge of the shape, drawing the outline as you go.

Tip: Consider each line that you put on the paper, so that you don't end up with a thick mass of lines. Constantly move your eye from the object to the paper.

Fill in the diamonds. Perhaps create a rainbow pattern.

3 ——————— Use the opposite page to draw trees. Use any materials you like. Start with the trunk and branches and then add the leaves or flowers.

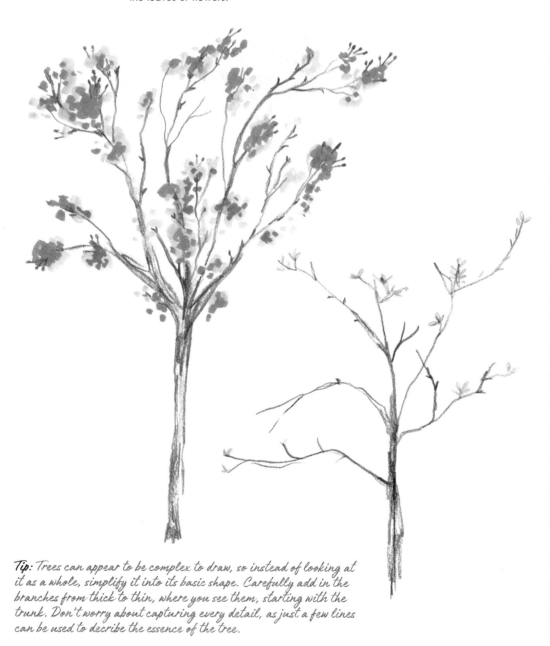

Tip: Trees can appear to be complex to draw, so instead of looking at it as a whole, simplify it into its basic shape. Carefully add in the branches from thick to thin, where you see them, starting with the trunk. Don't worry about capturing every detail, as just a few lines can be used to decribe the essence of the tree.

4 ——————— Draw the statue that the people are looking at.

5 —————— Fill the page with leaf shapes.

A colour wheel can be used to see the relationship between colours and helps with choosing palettes. Three of these colours – red, yellow and blue – are primary colours. Mix these together to make the rest of the colours.

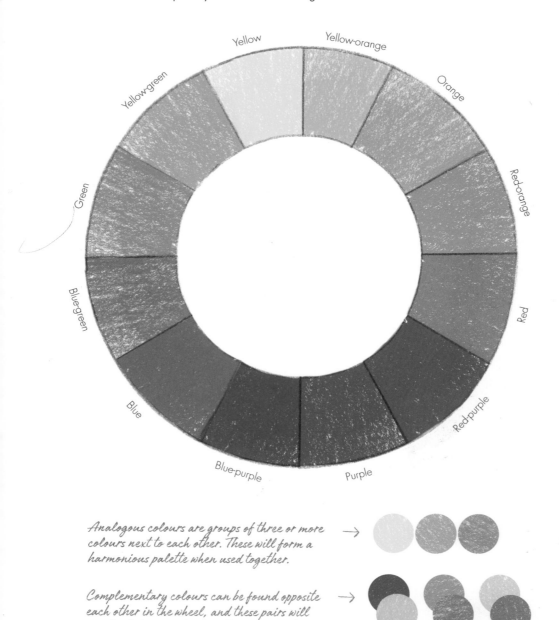

Analogous colours are groups of three or more colours next to each other. These will form a harmonious palette when used together.

Complementary colours can be found opposite each other in the wheel, and these pairs will create striking contrasts within your work.

Create your own colour wheel by adding in the colours. You can use any material you like, but it may be easier to mix colours with paints such as watercolour or gouache.

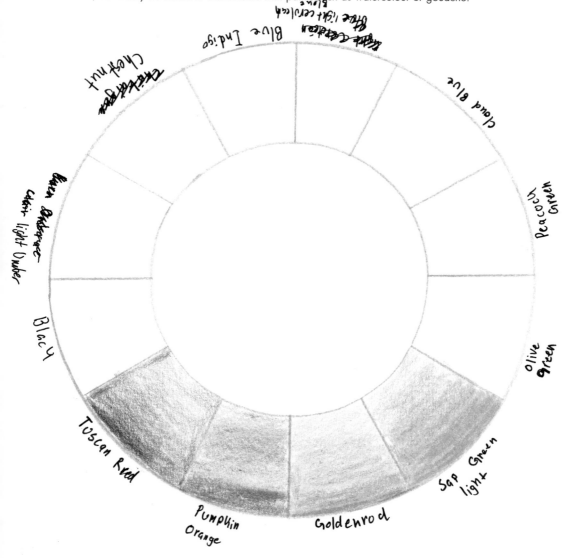

Chestnut
Blue Indigo
Blue
Blue light cerulean
Light cerulean
Cloud blue
Peacock Green
Burnt Umber
Colour light Umber
Black
Olive green
Tuscan Red
Sap Green light
Pumpkin Orange
Goldenrod

Tip: You may like to refer back to this colour wheel when you are completing other activities. It provides a useful reference when considering your palette choices.

7 ———— Draw the shoes you are wearing today.

8 ———— What is hiding in the reeds?

What is in the cups? Pencils? Flowers? Spoons?

What would be the one word you'd like to use to describe your year ahead? Write it here.

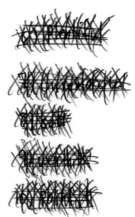

Create a 'blind drawing' on the opposite page. A blind drawing is when you draw an object without looking at your page. Choose a subject, and focus entirely on the object, following the shapes you see with your eye but moving your pen or pencil at the same time. If you can, use a continuous line, so draw without lifting your pen or pencil from the page.

Tip: Try to relax and not worry about how your drawing looks. This activity is more about learning to really look at an object rather than creating an accurate drawing.

12 ———— Continue the pattern. Try using different materials.

13 ———— Practise mark making: explore using white pastels and white pencils.

Draw different clothes on the hangers.

15

Create a rainbow. Perhaps use watercolour paint and let the colours bleed into each other.

Red

Orange

Yellow

Green

Blue

Indigo

Violet

Complete this flock of birds.

——————— Continue adding dashes to complete the pattern and fill the page.

Explore colours that look good together. Fill in the boxes
with the colours that you think work well as a set.

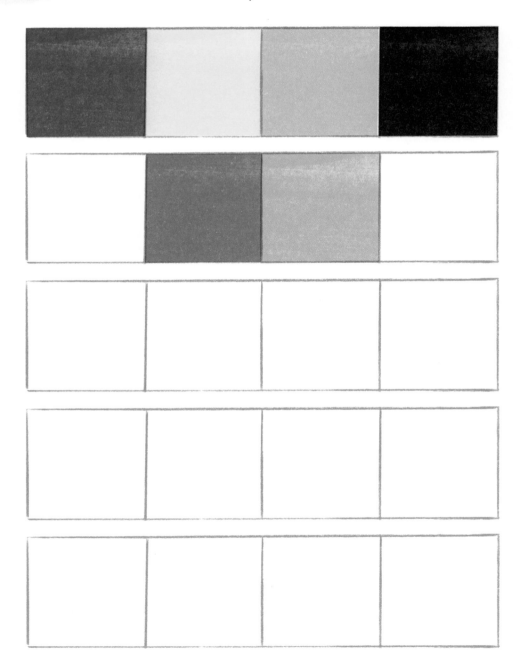

19 —————— Visit a museum or exhibition. Using coloured pencils, draw items that interest you. You may like to add information about the items alongside your drawings.

Tip: Drawing in public may feel intimidating, but with practise, you will forget all about the other people!

20

Fill the vase with flowers. You could cut the petals out of coloured paper or experiment with different materials.

21 ———— Explore mark making using the side of B pencils here. Tilt a pencil on it's side, and use your index finger to press down on the wooden area above the nib, and create soft, broad marks.

22 ———— Draw a tin or packet of food from your kitchen.

23

What is on the shelves? Books? Plants? Ornaments?

Colour or create a pattern.

25 ———————— Using watercolours, experiment with different brush strokes. Try applying different pressures to the brush and explore turning the brush as you move it.

26 ———————— Draw something that makes you happy.

———————— Fill the page with all the fruit you can think of.

28

Today, draw an everyday object and this time, pay particular attention to measuring the distances and angles by eye.

1. Roughly draw a horizontal line on the page. Then close one eye and hold up your pencil so that it forms a horizontal line along the side of the object. Carefully observe the angles made between the pencil and the object. Replicate these angles in your drawing.

2. Continue to draw the object, continually checking the angles by closing one eye and holding up a pencil either vertically or horizontally to your object. Observe the angles the object forms against these vertical and horizontal lines.

3. As you work your way around the drawing, notice how certain parts of the object relate to others. For example on this apple I have drawn a vertical line down from the stem, and by tilting my pencil as I hold it up to the apple, I can roughly work out the angle between the stem and the base of the fruit.

I can see that the edge of the apple drops down at roughly this angle from the horizontal line.

Horizontal line

Vertical line

Tip: With practise, you won't need to draw the lines and angles on the paper, but you should find it useful to continue to measure angles by eye.

Continue the diamond pattern using different materials.

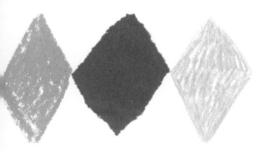

Create swatches of your coloured pencils. You can then refer to this page when you are choosing your colours.

mauve

vermillion

31

Find a photograph of a face. Turn it upside down, and draw it here. When we look at an image upside down, we see the tone and shape rather than a recogniseable face. This is a useful drawing technique as instead of drawing what we think a face should look like, we draw what we actually see.

Tip: Don't forget, your finished drawing will be upside down, so when you've finsihed, rotate the book to see it.

Fill the page with potted plants.

Fill the frames with artwork. Perhaps people, scenes, or a still life? If you like one of your mini paintings, you could recreate it as a larger scale painting.

34 ———— Fill the page with fast observational drawings of objects from around your home. You could use a fine liner pen for this, as it won't smudge whilst you draw.

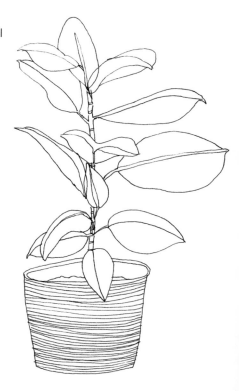

Tip: Don't worry about making mistakes, this exercise is about practising looking, and building your confidence. Your drawings can overlap, and you could continue drawing outside of this book.

35 —————— Draw a building or town.

Continue the pattern.

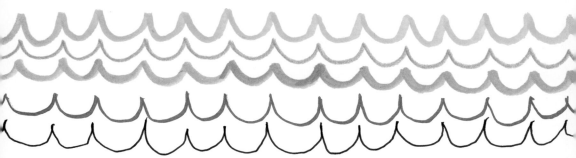

37 ———— Draw the animal these hooves belong to.

---

38 ———— Build your confidence by sharing your artwork. Create a piece of work (it can be as big or small as you like) and share it with anyone. Perhaps a friend, or family member, or even on social media. Note down how it made you feel.

Tip: Showing people what you've created can be scary, but it can be surprisingly rewarding. Try it!

39
————

Complete a line drawing of your bookcase using a fineliner pen or sharp pencil. For example, just draw the outlines of what you see, but draw the exact amount of books, carefully considering the relative widths of the spines, to make the drawing as accurate as possible.

Tip: Note the width of the first book and then use that as a guide for the rest of the widths. Perhaps the next book is twice the width of the first book.

40 ———————— Find an image that appeals to you. Glue it here if you can. Pick out the colours that you can see in the image, and paint colour swatches of them below, creating the colour palette of the image.

Tip: You could then take inspiration from this palette in your own drawing.

Draw a herd of animals in the forest clearing.

42 ———

Create a blind drawing on the opposite page, this time in colour. Choose what you are going to draw and select the colours you'll need for each of your objects. For every colour you see, draw in a continuous line, without lifting the pencil off the page. Then, switch colours and repeat.

Tip: Remember to look at the objects, tracing their outline with your eye, rather than the paper. Try choosing objects with patterns for an extra challenge.

43 The colour palette you choose can affect the mood of your drawing. Add colour swatches of cool colours below. What mood is created?

44 Draw an object from your home that was given to you as a gift.

45 ——————— Draw things you love about spring.

46 ——————— Practise mark making with a dry paintbrush and paint. You could use watered down acrylic, watercolour or ink. Either use a completely dry brush, or dip it in a very small amount of water, and experiment with making scratchy, textured marks. You may want to continue onto a new piece of paper.

Tip: Avoid using too much water or ink if you are worried about it soaking through the paper. You could also experiment on watercolour paper.

To make a drawing look three-dimensional you can add tone gradually, from light to dark. Use the space below to draw a simple obect using tone.

1. First, create swatches of 4 tones that you can see in the object from light to dark. You could use 3B–5B pencils for this, pressing harder to achieve the darker tones. You will refer back to these tones to whilst drawing.

Swatches:

1   2   3   4
Lightest   *Darkest*

2. Draw the whole shape of the object using your lightest tone (swatch 1). Simplify the object as much as possible so you are just focusing on the tone, not detail.

3. Add the medium tones, 2–3, into the areas where you see them on the object. You are building up the tone on the image from lightest to darkest.

4. Finally, add your darkest tone (swatch 4). You may want to sharpen your pencil to add the final dark details.

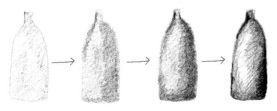

Tip: To help see the different tones, try squinting at the object.

Colour in the dots.

49

Fill the squares with different marks. You could try dashes, lines, spots, swirls and cross-hatches.

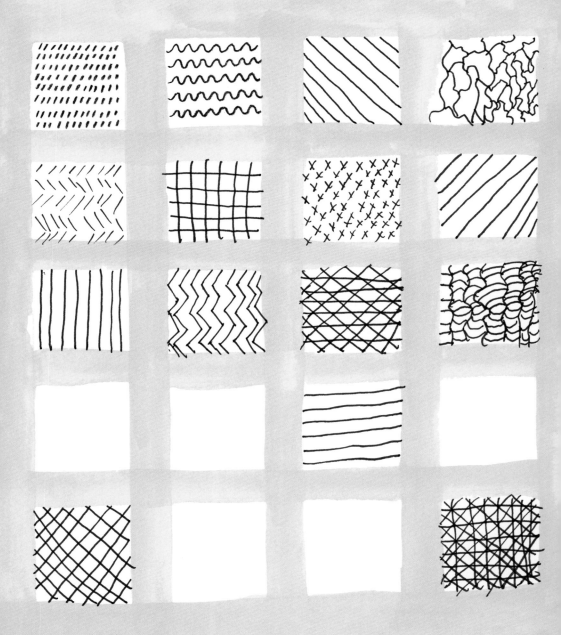

50

Draw a cold crisp day using only shades of blue. You could draw from your imagination, draw the view from your window, or even from a photograph.

Tip: Blue hues will have an effect on the feel of the drawing. It will help to emphasise the cold.

Today, explore blending colours using coloured pencils.
Use this space to experiment.

Tip: If you are using watercolour pencils, try adding water to your colours using a brush. Water can be used to blend these colours together.

Fill the page with interlocking coloured shapes.

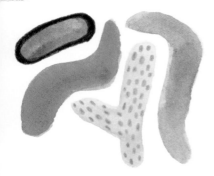

53 ———————

Sit outside, perhaps in a garden, a park or on a bench. Before you start drawing, look carefully at what you see around you for at least 5 minutes, and consider what interests you. Draw this below. Be sure to look at your surroundings as much as you do your paper; allow your eyes to repeatedly move from one to the other.

Tip: What can you hear? Perhaps you overhear a snippet of conversation that you'd like to include in your drawing to help capture the moment?

Use cut paper to create a simple pattern. Glue it in below.

Complete the shoal of fish.

Draw and write the postcard that you've always wanted to send.

Create a design or mini scene in each square. You could try using gouache here, as it works well on coloured backgrounds.

———————— Practise colour mixing with paints today.
Use watercolour or gouache, and explore
different colour combinations below.

The primary colours cannot be made from mixing other colours. These are red, blue and yellow.

You can use these 3 primary colours to mix secondary colours, and once you have these, you can make many more colours by mixing.

Primary

Secondary

Tip: Different hues of each colour will produce different results. For example, cold yellow + warm red will produce a different orange to a warm yellow + cold red. Explore this too.

59

Find a mirror and look at your reflection. Draw your face with both hands at once: hold a pencil in each hand and, starting at the top of your head, draw simultaneously using both pencils. Use the left side of this page to draw the left side of your reflection, using your left hand. Use the right side of this page to draw the right side of your reflection, with your right hand!

Tip: Keep both pencils moving at the same time, as your eyes move quickly from the left to the right of your reflection. It might be easier to concentrate on looking solely at your face, rather than the page you are drawing on.

Draw lots of birds just using simple shapes.

Complete a series of 3-minute drawings (as many as you can fit on this page) of an object or a person below. Set a timer, and, using a pencil, aim to get as much of the object drawn as possible in the time. Don't worry about whether you are creating a 'good drawing' – the purpose of this activity is to warm up, and it is a great exercise to practise every day.

Tip: It's fine if your drawings overlap each other – this could even create an interesting effect.

62

Create swatches of the paints in your watercolour palette. You can then refer to this page when you are choosing your colours.

cerulean
blue

emerald
green

When drawing out and about, try using a variety of different materials in one drawing. Use the page opposite.

Materials such as watercolour and wax pastel can cover large areas, and can be applied to the page quickly. You could use these first, to map out your main shapes. Here I have used them on the skin and jacket.

Details could be added using coloured pencil or a felt pen, as I have done here for the glasses, hair and collar.

Tip: If you use wax pastel, you could apply a layer of tracing paper on top of your page, fixing it with masking tape, to prevent your artwork from smudging.

Create a collage of coloured circles. You could use a variety of materials and add pattern details.

65

When choosing which pencils you will use for your drawing, note that pencils vary in how soft/hard they are. B pencils get increasingly soft and H pencils get increasingly hard. B pencils are better for shading as you can achieve a greater range from light to dark. Use the space below to explore the differences for yourself.

← Softness and blackness (good for shading)   Standard writing pencil ↓   Hardness → (good for precise lines)

6B   5B   4B   3B   2B   B   HB   H   2H

Tip: The greater the B value, the darker your tone will be, but also, the easier it will be to smudge. Try smudging 3B–6B pencil with your finger. Protect the opposite page by taping a sheet of tracing paper to this page.

66 ———————— Draw a plant outside. Perhaps you will choose to focus on one small element of the plant, and draw it close up.

67

Practise drawing the features on the faces here.
Draw the eyes about halfway down the face.

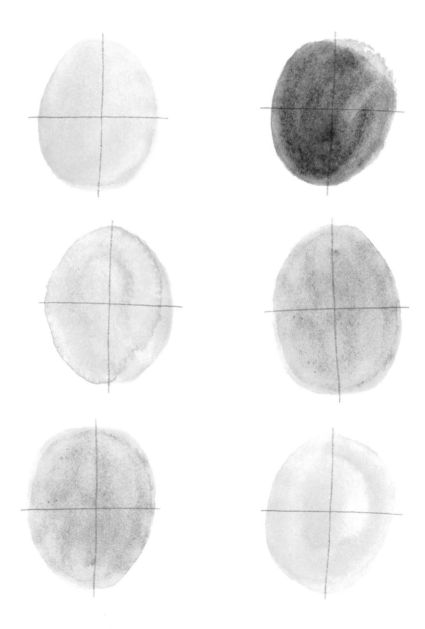

68 ———— Explore using a fine liner pen to create lines and marks.

Tip: Avoid pressing too firmly as this may cause damage to the nib.

69 ———— Use a white coloured pencil and a white gouache to draw snow-covered trees. Use the shape of the snow to suggest the shape of the trees. Consider how the snow adds weight to the tree.

70

What activities make you feel relaxed?
Draw or write them here.

71

Experiment with using wax crayons. You could try using
them as you would a pencil, and also on their side. If they
are water-soluble, add water to your drawing using a brush.

Spend 5–10 minutes creating a 'blind drawing' on the opposite page. This is when you look only at the object or scene you are drawing, not the paper or your drawing. It's a great technique to practise as it removes the fear of having a perfect drawing, and allows you to practise looking at how objects relate to each other in a space.

Tip: There is no pressure to have a finished drawing. Instead, it's about enjoying the process and getting used to looking at things carefully.

73

Today use pencils to create a tonal drawing. Adding tone (light and dark) helps to make your drawing look more three-dimensional. Start by choosing an everyday object.

1. Look carefully at your object. On the opposite page, draw a swatch of the lightest shade you can see, after white. You can use the paper as the lightest shade. Applying minimal pressure with the pencil will make it light. Next, add a swatch of the darkest shade you see. This will be used to outline the darkest areas and give the object a crisp edge. Add 2–3 medium tones that you can see in between, from light to dark.

Swatches:

1
Lightest
(Paper)

2

3

4

5
Darkest

2. Draw a light outline of the object.

3. Start by adding the tone from swatch 2 to the whole object. Then build up your tones from lightest to darkest where you see them. Try squinting at the object to better see the areas of tone.

4. Use an eraser to add highlight to the lightest areas by rubbing away the pencil. Use your darkest tone (swatch 5) to add definition to the darkest areas.

Tip: Remember, really look at the object. Draw what you see, rather than what you expect to see.

Swatches:

74 ──────── Draw a pencil using a fine liner pen. Move the pen slowly when drawing the straight lines.

75 ──────── Fill this area with horsehoes.

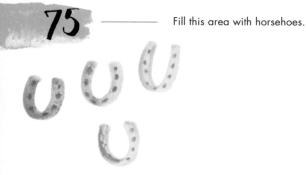

Colour or design some patterns between the lines.

77 ———————— Draw your desk space, or a table where you like to sit.

Tip: Perhaps cut and stick a piece of coloured paper to form the table top in your drawing. You could then draw objects on top of your table with a pen, or even create the entire drawing with collaged paper.

78

Using watercolour and a brush or water brush pen, practise controlling the thickness of the marks you make. Use this space to explore moving from thin to thick marks, and back again.

Apply minimal pressure on the brush to create a thin mark. Just the tip will be touching the paper.

To create a thicker line, gradually apply more pressure so that more of the brush is in contact with the paper.

Release the pressure again, gradually, to create a thinner mark.

Tip: Start slowly until you gain confidence using the brush.

Add colour.

Create a pattern using similar colours.

Tip: Refer back to your colour wheel in activity 6.

Add detail to the butterflies.

When you draw with paper you can create bold shapes and graphic designs. Create a drawing using just cut and torn paper. It could be an abstract image, or perhaps something from nature. Rather than concentrating on accuracy, enjoy exploring shape and colour, and perhaps sketch ideas in coloured pencil before you start.

Tip: Play with the composition of your design first, before you stick it down.

83 ——— Fill this area with life.

84 ——— Draw some windows.

Fill the page with drawings of apples. Experiment with different materials and styles.

86 ————— Using coloured pencils, write down or draw things that inspired you this month.

Draw and colour the leaves. Consider adding detail with sharp coloured pencils.

88 ———————— Draw an imaginary book cover.

89 ———————— What activities have you found most challenging so far? Why? How did you overcome the challenge?

90 ———— Add spring leaves to the trees.

91 ———— Draw a person you saw today, from memory.

Turn these paint splodges into animals.

What is the simplest way you can draw a chair? Explore below.

94

Today, practise drawing people. Although this may seem a more daunting challenge than drawing an object, we can apply the same skills – observing shape, measuring distances between parts and concentrating on what we can really see, as opposed to what we think we should be seeing.

A good place to practise drawing people is out and about. Visit the shops, public transport, or anywhere people congregate and you can comfortably sit and draw. Using a fine liner pen or pencil, create lots of observational drawings of people. Start with the outlines, rather than thinking about tone.

Tip: Don't be afraid, this is all about practise and you may make many drawings before you feel like you've cracked it!

Draw quickly but don't rush. Carefully observe how the person is sitting or standing. What are they wearing? Where are they looking? If you only have time to capture a small detail rather than the entire figure, that's fine!

Tip: It's useful to practise drawing people whenever you can. Perhaps take a small sketchbook with you on journeys, in case you get inspired to start drawing.

95

Using watercolour, explore the different widths of brush strokes you can make with just one brush. Fill the page. Vary the width of the stroke by alternating the pressure you apply to the brush.

For thinner strokes, hold the brush at a steeper angle, applying just a little pressure.

Apply more pressure to create thicker strokes.

96 ———————— Design a pattern or image using this grid.

97

Create a grid drawing. If you are drawing from a photograph, a great way to make an accurate copy is by using a grid. Here I have drawn a grid over an image of some leaves. Rather than looking at the leaves as a whole, just look at the angles and shapes you can see in each cell, and draw this in the corresponding cell opposite.

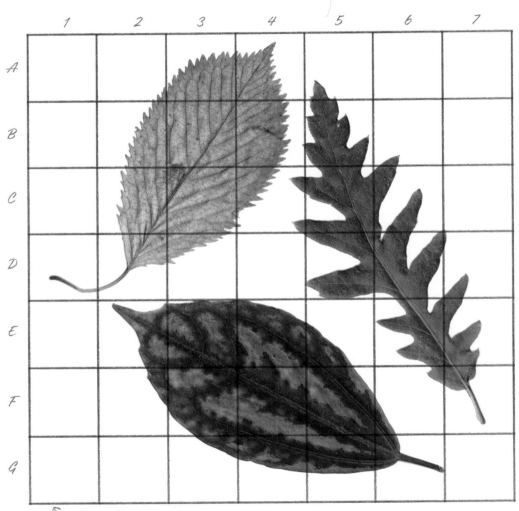

Numbering the cells means you can keep track of where you are. This cell is G1.

Tip: As well as looking at the shapes and angles at the edge of the leaf, look at the shapes made by the different colours inside each cell too.

	1	2	3	4	5	6	7
A							
B							
C							
D							
E							
F							
G							

98

Look at objects around your house.
Swatch all the colours you see.

Red flower

Tip: You may need to mix colours first in a mixing palette if using watercolour, or on to the paper if using coloured pencils.

99

Draw an object using the opposite hand to the one you usually draw with.

——————— Draw the faces of the cats.

Draw a sun using oranges and yellows.

102

Using B pencils, add tone to each of the boxes. There are lots of ways you can apply tone, and there is no right or wrong.

103 ——————— Draw things you love about autumn (fall).

104 ——————— Draw the rain.

Make a drawing of this flower below, using any materials you like.

Add foliage, berries or flowers.

107

Fill this quarter page with grey dots. Notice how some shades of grey are warm, and others are colder.

Tip: When you reach for a colour, consider which specific shade you are after – rather than just selecting any grey, perhaps choose a cool, blueish grey.

108

Explore different widths of fine liner pen here.

0.25 mm

0.45 mm

0.2 mm

109

Make a drawing from life using coloured lines. Choose your colours, then quickly draw your subject using a different line colour for each colour you see.

Tip: If you are drawing a person, and they move, that's OK! Just adapt your drawing and redraw your line – there's no need to erase any lines.

Design a pattern on the snake.

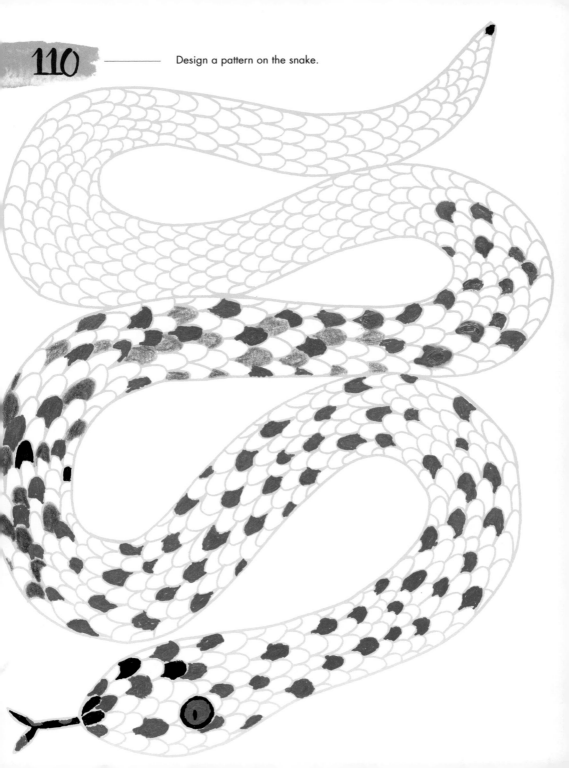

Add tone to the boxes. You can use any colour and material you like.

Tip: Consider where your light source is on each box — perhaps it's coming from a different direction on each box. Which sides are in shadow?

112 ———— Different materials can mimic the look of fur or hair. Try creating **hair** and fur textures below, for example using pastel rubbings or tight **lines**.

113 ———— Continue drawing circles with a fine liner pen, then colour in the shapes using coloured pencils.

114

Practise drawing people today. Use pencil or pen and work quickly, trying to capture the personality of the person in your drawing. What are they wearing? What do you find interesting about them?

115 ———— Explore using the sharper end of a wax pastel to create marks.

/ /

116 ———— Draw one of your favourite belongings.

117

Create repeat patterns within the stripes. You could use cut paper, or any material you like.

118

Make quick sketches of an animal using a fine liner pen. Spend just a few seconds on each drawing, and fill the page with your observational drawings.

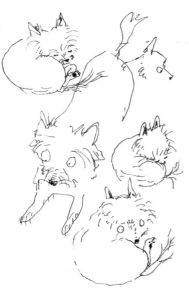

Tip: Instead of drawing an animal in real life, you could watch videos of animals online and capture them as they move.

119

Choose an object. Draw it 4 times, each time in a more abstract style. Look carefully at the object for drawing 1. Then for each subsequent drawing, simplify the elements you have drawn previously.

1.

2.

3.

4.

Tip: Exaggerate the elements you liked in your previous drawings. Simplify the shapes and marks. Perhaps the drawings get increasingly loose.

The colour palettes you choose can affect the mood of your drawing. Create your own colour palettes to describe each mood below. There isn't a right or wrong answer, as it's about how the colours make *you* feel. Use any material you like.

Calm

Happy

Enchanting

Romantic

Natural

Sombre

Energetic

Tip: If you don't have the exact colour, mix colours together. Consider how you can use these palettes in your future artworks.

Design labels and add details to the bottles. You could use coloured paper to create bold, graphic shapes.

Add colour to the leaves.

123 ——————— Spend 15 minutes creating a blind drawing. Choose an everyday scene, perhaps some objects in your kitchen. Look carefully at how each object relates to another.

124

Using a limited amount of coloured pencils, draw people out and about, spending just a few seconds on each drawing. Sometimes you may only have time to draw a key detail, such as hair or shoes, before they move away. Practising these drawings will help build your confidence and you will also learn what you are naturally drawn to when sketching.

Tip: Having just a few coloured pencils available means that you won't be overthinking your colour choices, and will instead be capturing the details you can see.

Draw a flock of birds. Are they close or near?

126 ———— Fill the space with stars.

127 ———— Draw some bicycles. These can seem complicated to draw, so break them down into their simplest shapes.

Design a tiled floor.

129

Complete a tonal drawing of an everyday object, building up the tone of the drawing from light to dark. You could use 3B–7B pencils, and an eraser to add highlights.

Tip: Try holding the pencil loosely at the top. If you are concerned about your page smudging, tape a sheet of tracing paper over it.

Add stripes or patterns.

131

Put on some relaxing, wordless music – perhaps calming meditation track or something classical. Choose a material to work with, perhaps coloured pencils or wax pastels. Draw below as you listen to the music.

Tip: This could be a page of abstract doodles. Enjoy the experience of creating whilst listening to the sounds.

Use swatches of paper to create colour palettes.

Draw a person sat in a chair. This could be somebody you know at home, or a stranger in a cafe. Start by applying the blocks of colour – the clothing, hair, seat and face. Then add detail with a sharp coloured pencil or fine liner pen.

Tip: If you are nervous about drawing on to your blocks of colour, tape a layer of tracing paper to on top of your page, and draw your line details on this layer instead. You will be able to see your coloured blocks below.

Fill the page with coloured triangles. Use any material you like.

135

Practise drawing circles using a fine liner pen. Start slowly, using the guides, then continue practising below.

136 ——————— The colour palette you choose can affect the mood of your drawing. Add colour swatches of warm colours below. What mood is created?

137 ——————— Explore using the blunt end of a wax pastel to create marks.

138

Add colour to the stars.

139 ——————— Draw a feather. Choose one with interesting colours.

140

Fill the grid with colour. Think carefully about which colours you use, so that all adjacent colours look good together.

Fill the page with drawings of pencils. Experiment with different materials and styles.

Today, draw an object using wax pastels on the opposite page.

1. Choose your lightest colour and, holding your pastel loosely, use the side of the nib to roughly draw your object.

2. Begin adding colour, pressing harder for darker areas of tone. Use the side of the nib to cover larger areas.

Tip: Enjoy the loose texture and rough-and-ready nature of the wax pastels – don't worry too much about making precise marks.

3. Continue to build colour and tone from light to dark. Use the finer point of the wax pastel to create areas of definition.

4. Finally, use your darkest tone to add definition. Be sparing with black, and don't be afraid to leave areas undefined.

143 ——————

Create a drawing that reminds you of your favourite trip away. This could be a mix of graphic and abstract, just focusing on the key colours and imagery. Or perhaps a more detailed drawing.

144 —————— Draw what is under the sea.

145 —————— Call up a friend. Ask them what their favourite place to visit is. Draw it!

Use this page to create doodles which explore using different materials.

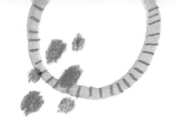

Design the mugs.

148

Complete a grid drawing here using a photograph of a scene and creating your own grid.

Choose an image you'd like to draw – perhaps from a newspaper or magazine.

Using a fine liner pen, draw a horizontal line at the bottom of the area you'd like to include in your drawing. Draw a vertical line on the left side of the area.

Then, draw lines horizontally and then vertically, an equal distance apart, so that you make square cells. Label your grid with numbers and letters.

Draw another grid on the opposite page, in pencil. Your grid doesn't have to be the same size, just make sure it has the same amount of columns and lines, and that the cells are square.

Draw what you see in each cell, focusing on the shapes and negative space.

Tip: The more cells that make up your grid, the more accurate your drawing will be, as you can focus in greater detail. Draw the grid in light pencil so that at the end it is no longer visible.

Continue the pattern using coloured pencils.

Draw the earth from 3 different views.

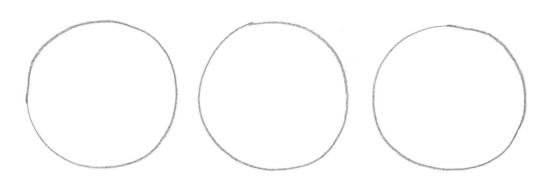

Before drawing a scene, it can be useful to draw a thumbnail (small sketch) to test your composition works, and also to help plan the drawing. These can be drawn quickly and roughly using a pencil. You could even use it to test colours that may work together in your drawing. Draw some thumbnail sketches of scenes here.

Swatch all the colours you can see in a fire.

Add faces and hair to the crowd.

Continue drawing a leaf pattern until you fill the page.

155

Add leaves to these palms. You could use wax pastels.

Tip: Explore different brushes and speeds of painting — moving your brush slowly and quickly to alter the effect.

Slow

Fast

157

Sketch a person's face. Ask somebody to sit still for you for about 10 minutes whilst you draw them. Begin with a rough pencil sketch, and then observe the areas of tone you can see, adding cross-hatching.

Tip: Squinting your eyes makes it easier to see the areas of tone. Add tone from light to dark, finishing off by using an eraser on the highlights, and a sharp, hard pencil on the darkest areas.

Fill a page with doodles as soon as you wake up. How are you feeling now, and about the day ahead? What are you looking forward to?

Add designs to the flowers.

Draw a warm day using only shades of red and orange.
You could draw from your imagination, draw outside or
even from a photograph.

Create a patchwork of circles using a range of materials.

Fill the page with imaginary plants.
Experiment with different materials and styles.

163 ———— Find a pattern that you like. Draw it here using fine liner pens.

Tip: If the pattern is very complex, begin by looking at each individual element – how do they interact with each other?

164

Apply watercolour to a wet brush and make small strokes from left to right. Notice how the colour gradually fades as you move across the page.

165 —————— Draw a journey you have made recently.

——————— Fill the pot. Perhaps with pencils.

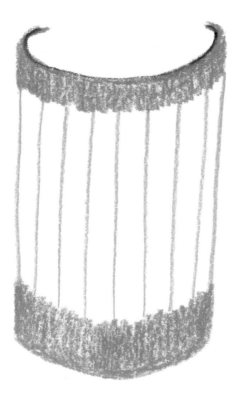

167

Drawing out and about can feel intimidating. Today, when in a cafe, library or just outside, draw a small part of the room or scene which you feel comfortable looking at. In the space below, draw quickly and freely, focusing on getting the lines down on the paper.

Tip: You could look up, and draw what you see above you – perhaps an interesting lamp? This is a good activity to do at the beginning of a drawing session out and about, as it will help build your confidence and put you ease when drawing in public.

Draw what the people are looking at.

You can create tone in many different ways, with lots of different materials. Use the materials suggested below to create tonal drawings of spheres in the boxes on this page. Observe a round object as you draw, such as a ball or an orange.

Coloured pencil:
Follow the curve of the sphere, pressing harder as you move to the parts of the sphere that would be darkest.

Tip: Consider where your light source is coming from.

Pencil:
Rub the side of the nib onto the paper to create tone. Start by pressing lightly, for the lightest tone, and then gradually build tone from light to dark by pressing harder.

Watercolour paint:
Start by mixing one colour with lots of water and paint a flat circle out of your lightest tone. Build up the tone using layers of gradually more intense colour, allowing layers to dry in between. You could use a tissue to dab away colour from the lightest areas.

Brush tip pen:
Build up layer by layer. The more layers you apply to an area, the darker it will be. Follow the circular shape with the brush as you go.

Ink pen:
There are many ways to build tone with an ink pen, but you could try cross-hatching. Add more hatching to the areas which are darkest. It may be easiest to start from the darkest point, and grow the cross-hatching outwards.

170

Your drawings don't need to be very complicated. Find an object or group of objects with shapes that interest you, and draw them in their simplest form.

Focus on what makes the objects identifiable. For example, with these bottles, it is their distinctive shape. Line isn't always necessary, and you can draw shapes just using blocks of colour.

Fill the page with white stars using a variety of materials.

172 ———————— Draw things you love about the winter.

173 ———————— Use this area to practise making long brush strokes.

174 ———————— List all the ways in which you are creative.

175 ———————— Draw the rest of the scene.

176

Draw the 'negative space' around a simple object. Only look at the space and shape around an object, rather than looking at the object itself. Observing the negative space is another tool we can use to help us draw an accurate shape. It helps to focus the mind on the angles around the shape, rather than worrying too much about drawing a particular object.

Tip: You can use the side of a B pencil for this, to create a thick line.

Turn the splodges into animals.

Consider the positions of the facial features when drawing a face. The eyes and ears are roughly halfway down the face. Use the space below to practise drawing a face using an axis as a guide. Follow these steps below, and draw as many faces as you like. You could look at photographs for reference.

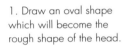

1. Draw an oval shape which will become the rough shape of the head.

2. Add a skin tone

3. Draw an axis, so that the lines cross in the middle of the face.

4. Draw the edge of the face and add the features.

179 ———————— Fill this area with different shapes.

180 ———————— Draw a car in the simplest way you can, using just a few lines or marks. Perhaps use cut paper to form the shape.

181 ———— Complete the mountain scene.

182 ———— What have you enjoyed drawing so far?

183 —————— Draw the moon using silvers, greys and blues.

184 ———————— Continue creating circles in any material you like, perhaps also cut from paper or patterns that you have found.

185 Draw shapes of leaves, real or imaginary. Perhaps they overlap to form a pattern.

Put on some sounds from the natural world – perhaps the sound of the rain, or a rainforest, which can be found by searching online. Choose a material to work with, perhaps coloured pencils or wax pastels. Draw below as you listen to the sounds.

Tip: This could be a page of abstract doodles or a scene. Enjoy the experience of creating whilst listening to the sounds. How do they make you feel?

Use each square to experiment with pattern and mark making.

188 ———————— Fill this quarter page with blue dots. Notice how some shades are warm, and others cold.

189 ———————— Which of your drawings are you most proud of so far?

190 ————— Write down some ideas as to how you can be more creative in your everyday life.

191 ————— Add the flowers.

Add colour to the fish.

Draw the refection of your face as you see it in a spoon.

194 — Doodling can be a great way to express yourself and also to relax. Fill this area with doodles.

195 — Create autumnal gradients on these leaves.

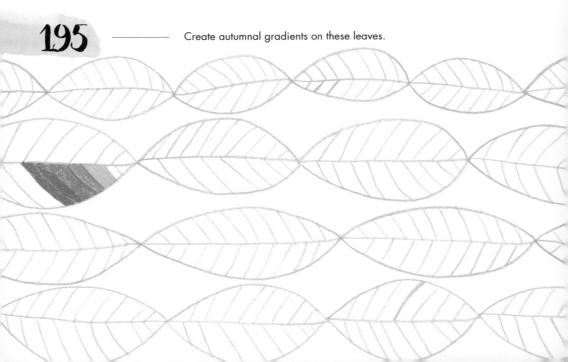

196 ———— Draw something you remember seeing today.

197 ———— What inspires you to draw?

1. Roughly draw the shapes that you see for the whole object or scene.

4. Add detail using line.

2. Then look carefully at your rough sketch, checking and measuring the distances between all of the edges.

3. Add colour in blocks.

——————— Fill the page with lines.

Fill the glasses.

Create a drawing using collaged paper today. Choose your subject, which could be anything that inspires you. Draw with the scissors rather than a pencil, and cut the paper as you observe the shape. Start with a rough shape and then refine with the scissors.

Tip: You could use coloured pencils to add detail and tone to your paper shape.

202 ———— Hold an object in one hand, and a pen or pencil in the other. Without looking at it, draw what you feel. What does the texture feel like, and the shape?

Tip: This may not end up looking much like your object, but might give a sense of the essence of it, and how you interpret it.

203

Practise drawing circles using different materials. Start slowly so you can control the direction of the line.

Design a tiled floor or mosaic.

205

Today, create a complementary colour scale. Complementary colours are those found opposite each other on the colour wheel. Mixing two complementary colours together, by gradually adding more of one colour to the other, will create a complementary scale. Any colours taken from this scale will give you a cohesive palette, when used together in a drawing.

1. Start by choosing 2 complementary colours from your colour wheel. Create swatches of them on the page opposite. Use watercolour, gouache, or even acrylic if you have it.

2. Gradually mix a little bit of one colour into the other, creating a swatch each time you mix a new colour. You may want to mix the colours in a clean mixing palette.

Browns and blacks are made from mixing complementary colours.

3. Repeat for the other pairs of complementary colours. You may want to work vertically down the page, so you have enough room.

Tip: You could then apply these palettes to drawings, and be confident all the colours in each complementary scale will work well together. Be selective – perhaps just choose 2 or 3 colours from each scale to create a drawing.

206 ——— Sometimes, drawing on coloured paper can be less intimidating than a blank white page. Fill the area with drawings.

207 ——— Create a scene around this branch.

208 ———— What is on the shelf?

209 ———— Hair always grows in a particular direction, so when you are drawing it, look for the direction it is growing. Practise drawing hair here.

210

Fill the room with plants. Perhaps design a floor too.

Continue the pattern, using wax pastels.

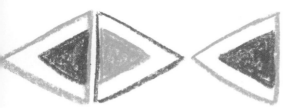

212

Using coloured pencils, add colour to the shapes so that where they overlap, they create a new colour.

Tip: To create the mixed hue, you may need to apply a few layers of each colour.

213 ———— Draw a close-up of an egg. Notice all the different colours and marks.

214 ———— Look closely at your hand. Swatch all the colours you can see.

215 ———————

Draw a friend or family member from life. You could use pencils, and start by roughly drawing the shape of the head. Then mark where the features on the face are, being careful to measure the distance beween each part of the face. Add areas of tone where you see it, but work quickly and don't worry too much about detail.

216

Using fine liner pens, explore ways of adding tone to each of the boxes. You could use different nib sizes.

—————

Today, create an analogous palette. Analogous colours are those found alongside each other on the colour wheel. Mixing two or three analogous colours together, by gradually adding more of one colour to another, will create a palette of harmonious hues. Any colours taken from this palette will go well together in a drawing.

1. Using paint, choose any 3 colours which are next to each other on a colour wheel. Create swatches of these colours.

2. Mix these colours together in as many ways as you can. You can also use white. There is an enormous number of possible new colours that you can create, by mixing the colours in different quantities. Fill the opposite page with swatches.

3. You can also introduce very small amounts of complementary colours to your colour mixing too, as these new colours will also work well in your palette.

Tip: You could then apply a selection of colours from this palette to a drawing or pattern, and be confident that any of the colours you have created on the page will work well together. Perhaps circle 5 or 6 colours from this palette that you'd like to use to create an image.

218 ———— Draw what is growing beneath the ground.

219 ———— From memory, draw a friend from your childhood.

220

Explore controlling the thickness of your marks when using a brush or water brush pen and watercolour. Create lines of loops.

Apply pressure as you move the brush down, to create a thicker mark.

Begin here, with a thin mark.

Gradually relieve pressure to create a thinner line as you loop around and repeat.

Tip: Keep your wrist loose and relaxed, and aim to get in to a rhythm as you draw.

221 ——————— What are you looking forward to tomorrow?
Draw it below.

222 ——————— Draw a desert island.

223 ——— Draw the contents of the bottles.

Fill the page with faces in profile.

Fill the page with drawings of oranges. Experiment with different materials and styles.

226 ———————— Fill this quarter with objects that are all your favourite colour.

227 ———————— What inspired you today? What did you see that made you want to draw?

228 ———— Add colour to the fish.

229 ———— What is your favourite thing to draw? Draw it here.

Create a page of birds.

231

Draw an everyday object using watercolour paint.
Sketch the shape in coloured pencil first. You could
also use colouring pencil once you've finished painting,
to add definition.

Tip: Build up your colour from light to dark and allow the paint to dry between layers.

232

Draw an object so it looks three-dimensional using greyscale tones. Choose an object – it could be as simple or complex as you like. Also choose the material you would like to use. This could be pencil, paint, cut paper, or even a combination all of these.

Using whichever materials you have chosen, create swatches of the tones you can see, from light to dark.

1   2   3   4   5

1. Draw a light outline of your object.

2. Apply swatch 1 to the entire shape.

3. Build up the tone using swatches 2, 3 and 4.

4. Continue adding tone from light to dark.

5. Add the very darkest tone last (swatch 5), in small areas.

6. Perhaps add a shadow using one of your midtones (swatches 3 or 4).

Tip: Squint your eyes to help identify light and dark tones.

233

Draw the negative space around a complex object such as a plant. Only observe and draw the space and shape around the object, rather than looking at the object itself.

Tip: There may be negative shapes inside the object too, such as between leaves or branches. Be sure to draw this too.

234 ——————— Fill this area with drawings of furniture.

235 ——————— Draw an animal using only colour. Avoid using any black.

236

Spend just 3 minutes on a drawing today. Draw some hands. As you draw, focus most of your attention on the hands, rather than the paper. If you have completed a drawing and have time remaining within the 3 minutes, check and correct the angles, drawing straight on top of previous lines.

237

Fill the page with coloured triangles.
Consider which colours look appealing
alongside each other. Perhaps you will
discover new combinations you like.

238 ——————— Arrange a still life scene. This could include a vase of flowers, some fruit, or anything else you like. Draw it below, in colour. You could use watercolours.

Tip: Choose objects with simple shapes for a less complex drawing. You could sketch out the objects in relation to each other first, or, for a looser, more organic piece, you could draw freely and not worry so much about accuracy.

Explore using different materials alongside and on top of each other. Create abstract circle shapes.

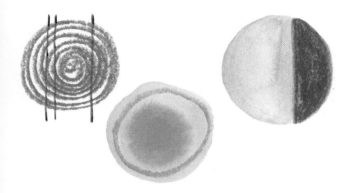

240 ———— Draw an image from your favourite book.
Perhaps visualise a phrase that inspires you.

241 ———— Use a different material to colour each of the grapes.

242

Draw skies below. Consider different weather conditions. Where do you see the light and dark?

Fill the bowl.

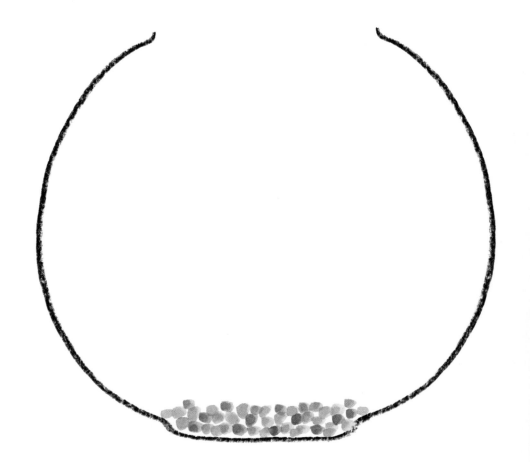

244

Make colour palettes using swatches of coloured paper. Consider shapes and details which may also work well with the colours to create a piece of artwork. Perhaps make each palette into it's own abstract drawing.

Draw a friend or family member (or even someone in a cafe) using tone in just one colour. Using paint, perhaps watercolour, draw the shapes as a block using your lightest tone first, and then build the tone in blocks from light to dark. Finally, add detail using a sharp pencil.

Tip: If drawing a friend, you could draw each other at the same time!

246 ——— Draw some footprints.

247 ——— Create lines of pattern using wax pastels.

248 ———— Create a pattern using complementary colours.

Tip: See activity 6 for your colour wheel.

249 ———— Add designs to the socks.

250 —————— Draw the rest of the forest scene.

251 —————— Write down 3 things you admire about other people's artwork.

Fill the page with drawings of shells.

253

Put the hand you don't draw with on the table. Draw it below. Look carefully at the negative shapes between the fingers, the position of the knuckles and the shapes of the nails.

Tip: Hands are difficult to draw, but you can practise drawing your own whenever you like, as they are right there!

254

Today, try creating a tonal drawing using the colour of a piece of fruit.

1. Look carefully at the fruit. On the opposite page, paint or colour a swatch of the lightest tone you can see. Then paint or colour a swatch of the darkest, and 2–3 medium tones you can see in between, from light to dark. Look carefully at which colours you can see.

Swatches:

1
Lightest

2

3

4
Darkest

2. Draw the whole shape of the fruit using your lightest tone.

3. Add the medium tones, 2–3, into the areas where you see them on the fruit. You are building up the image from lightest tone to darkest.

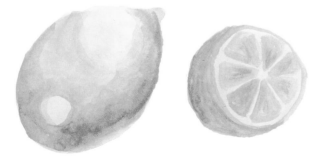

4. Add your darkest tones, and then add detail using sharp coloured pencils. You could also add the shadow to the fruit. Avoid using black, instead look carefully at what colour the shadows really are.

Tip: Remember to try squinting to help to see the different tones.

Swatches:

255

Complete a grid drawing here, but this time, use a photograph of a face. Rather than drawing a grid straight on to the photo, you could create a photocopy, or draw your grid on tracing paper and attach it over the top of your photo. Remember to make sure your grid on the photograph is proportionally the same as the grid you draw below. The simplest way to do this is to make sure all your cells are square, and that there are the same number of lines and columns.

Tip: A face may seem more tricky to draw, but remember to just look at each cell in your grid individually, and draw the shapes and space you see in each cell. If you are finding it tricky, turn the photo, and the book, and draw the image upside down.

Put pairs of colours you like together here. You could use any material you like, such as torn paper, or even patterns you like, cut from magazines or printed out.

 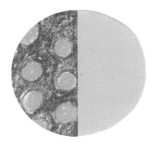

257

Add designs to the vases.

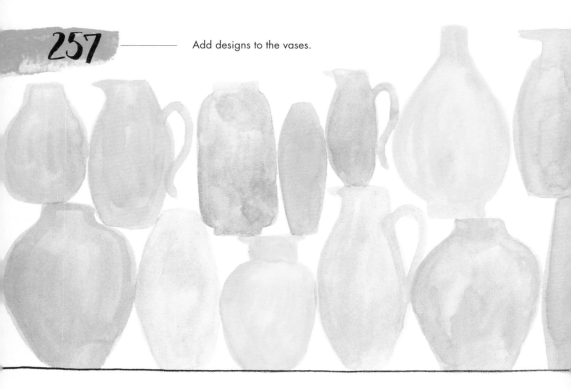

258

Draw the moon from 3 angles.

259 ———

To help find interesting compositions, you can use your hands as a viewfinder.

Using your fingers and thumb, create a rectangle. Hold it out in front of you, and move it around the room – what you see through the rectangle will be your composition. It may help to close one eye as you look through.

When you find a composition you like, create a thumbnail sketch below.

Move your thumbs closer together to change the cropping of your composition.

Tip: This is a great tool to use when choosing a subject matter when you're out and about. There can be an overwhelming amount to look at, so using your viewfinder helps to simplify and be selective.

260 ———————— Choose a small object or piece of furniture in your house. Draw it 10 times below. You could try many different materials, or just stick with one. Perhaps draw it from different angles.

Fill the design with neutral tones.

Add autumn (fall) leaves to the trees.

263

What would sand look like if you drew it close-up?

264

Create an abstract drawing of an object. What makes it identifiable? Use any material, and make it as simple or complex as you like.

Tip: Gouache paint is great for producing bold colour.

265

Write 3 things you like about your own drawings.

_____

_____

_____

_____

_____

_____

_____

_____

266

Create 3 colour blends. Start by painting 2 different watercolour colours at each end of the grid. Create a gradual blend of the 2 colours my mixing them together. Start with colour 1, and gradually add more of colour 2.

Colour 1   Colour 2

Blend 1

Blend 2

Blend 3

Tip: You may want to mix your colours in a mixing palette first.

Continue exploring wax pastels below.

268 —————— Continue the pattern.

269 ———— Draw the negative shape between a row of bottles.

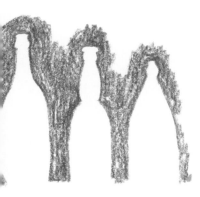

270 ———— Don't be afraid to ruin or 'go wrong' with a drawing as practise and also enjoying the process are as important as the end result. Draw something here which you struggle with, for example hands or faces. Try not to use an eraser, allow the mistakes to happen. Enjoy taking the time to create.

271

Begin a drawing of a building by focusing on the negative space around the structure. This might be the sky, so start by just drawing the shape the sky makes around the building. Then add details to your buildings.

Tip: You could leave the building itself white (using the colour of the paper).

272

Create a tonal drawing of a vegetable using coloured pencils. Start by creating swatches of your tones, using the white of the paper as your lightest tone. You can choose a variety of different colours, being sure to apply them to your drawing from light to dark.

Swatches:

Tip: Try using the side of the pencil nib to shade large areas. For the lightest parts – the highlights – use an eraser to reveal the clean, white paper.

273

Explore controlling the thickness of your marks when using a brush or water brush pen and watercolour. Create lines of loops.

Apply pressure as you loop the brush around, to create a thicker mark.

Begin here →

Create a thick downwards stroke, then relieve pressure as you start to curve the line.

Loop around and repeat.

Tip: Water brush pens are a good tool for this as the brush doesn't dry out, meaning your marks will be smooth.

274

Practise drawing bare feet. Feet, like hands, can be tricky.
Look carefully at the angles and distances you can see,
rather than drawing what you expect to see.

*Tip: If you are drawing with pencils, put a spare sheet of
paper beneath your hand as you draw, to avoid smudging.*

275 ———— Complete a drawing of this flower using the grid. Look at the angles, colours and shapes you can see in each cell in the grid, and copy it into the corresponding grid opposite. Begin by drawing the outline, then once you are happy, add colour. You could use coloured pencils for this, as you can achieve detail with the sharp point.

Tip: If part of your drawing doesn't look quite right, check that the shapes you have drawn in each cell match the shapes in the image above.

	1	2	3	4	5	6	7
A							
B							
C							
D							
E							
F							
G							

——————— What is the simplest way you can draw a tree? Explore below.

277

Create a pattern here. You may want to draw more elements and shapes into the design.

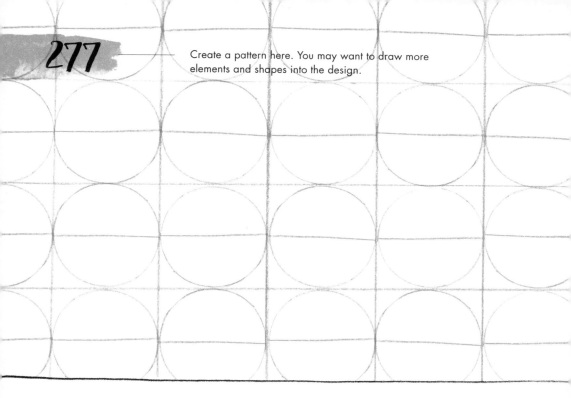

278

Today, share some of your artwork with someone. This could be online, or in real life. Ask them what they like about your artwork. Write what they say here.

279

Create a page of studies of people's ears. Ears are complicated shapes, so it's useful to practise drawing them on their own before drawing a whole face. Look closely at the dark and light areas of tone, and be careful to draw what you see, rather than what you expect to see. Carefully observe the angles, and start off keeping your sketches simple.

Tip: You could draw people's ears on trains or perhaps when someone in your household is watching TV. You can even practise by looking at photographs, but draw from life when possible.

Continue the pattern.

281

Today, complete drawing studies of an animal. Perhaps draw a pet, a friend's pet, some wild birds or even an animal from an online video. You may want to use pencil or coloured pencils for this activity, as you can work quickly with them and vary the tone depending on how hard you press.

1. Begin by drawing fast sketches of the animal. These shouldn't take more than 30 seconds each. Concentrate on capturing the form of the animal, and the size of the parts of the body in relation to each other.

2. Continue making drawings of the animal. Introduce tone, and try using thicker lines to add weight to your subject. Squint your eyes to observe the darkest areas of the animal. If your animal has fur, notice the direction of the hairs and move your pencil in the same direction.

Tip: Don't worry too much about reaching a final stage with these drawings. Just enjoy drawing the form of the animal, and really looking at your subject.

282

Choose an object and fill a page with blind drawings of it. Continue to observe the object and draw, only looking at the page when you have finished each drawing.

Tip: Try it in colour too. Have all your pencils ready, and try not to be tempted to look at the page whilst you swap colours!

Add flowers to the bunch.

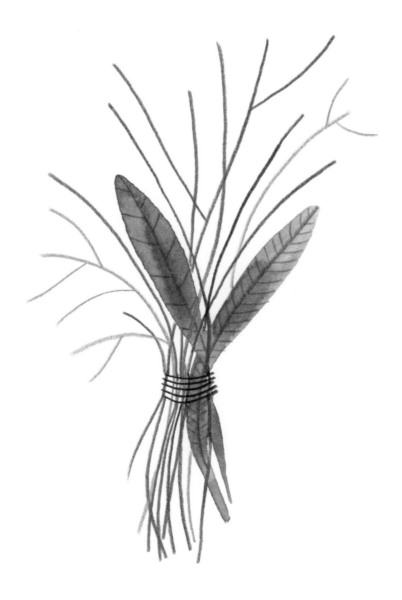

284

Using watercolour, create a simple drawing of a bowl using monochromatic colours, and draw it's contents using complementary colours.

Monochromatic colours are tones of just one colour – different intensities of the same hue. To create monochromatic tones, choose your base tone, and then add more white or slightly more black to make tones lighter or darker.

Monochromatic colour tones

Complementary colours are those which appear directly opposite each other on the colour wheel.

Complementary colours

1. Choose a colour for your bowl, and draw it using monochromatic colour tones. Perhaps create a pattern.

2. Draw the contents of the bowl using the complementary colour of the colour you have chosen for the bowl. For example, if you have chosen a blue bowl, the contents could be oranges. A red bowl could have green contents, such as apples.

3. Finish off the drawing with extra details.

Tip: Using a monochromatic colour scheme can make your drawing cohesive and you can be sure your colours will go well together. Using complementary colours can create a very striking drawing due to the high contrast.

285

Fill this quarter page with green dots.

Tip: When you think of an object as being green, consider how many different shades of green there are – sap green, grass green, cold and warm. Instead of thinking about a leaf being green, think about what type of green it is.

286

Using the opposite hand to the one you usually draw with, draw your reflection in a mirror.

Create some images below, where you are using negative space within your drawing. For example, to draw a white piece of clothing, you could focus on the negative space around the clothes, rather than the clothes themselves.

Fill this page with drawings of noses.
Consider the variety of sizes and shapes.

Turn these paint splodges into animals.

Turn the book on its side and fill the page with lampshade designs.

Add birds to the lines.

Using coloured pencils, draw an animal as it moves around, perhaps a pet or a bird. Capture the key details as quickly as you can, and as soon as the animal changes position, start a new drawing.

Tip: Spend as much time looking at the subject as you can, with just the occasional glance down at the paper. This is where the skills learnt whilst practising blind drawing come in handy, as you will need to gather as much information in each moment as possible.

Use the space below to draw thumbnail sketches. These can be used before you start a final drawing, to quickly test whether a composition is working, and adjust it if it isn't. There's no need for detail here, they can be very simple as they are just a way of jotting down ideas.

Tip: Thumbnails can be used before any kind of drawing — potraits, landscapes, imaginary or observational. Doing a quick, rough sketch should be the first thing you do before starting a sustained piece of drawing, as it's the time to spot any glaring issues with composition. After you've drawn your thumbnail, take a step back and check the balance. Are there any awkward shapes? If it doesn't feel quite right, sketch a different composition.

Draw an alphabet of items. Start from A, then B . . . all the way to Z, drawing an object for each letter.

295

Today, try a painting – perhaps use gouache or watercolour. Choose a subject, it could be a plant, some fruit or anything you are interested in drawing. Start by looking carefully at the subject, and for each of the colours you see, swatch your 4–6 tones from light to dark. Draw your subject in paint, working from the lightest to the darkest tones. You may find it helpful to sketch a rough outline and then paint a base for the entire shape first, using one of your lightest swatches.

Swatches:

Tip: If using gouache or watercolour, you may like to blend your tones together, or perhaps leave the blocks of tone unblended, for a more graphic effect.

296 ———— Fill the page with pebbles.

297

Create a line drawing here of a corner in your home using a coloured line, instead of black or grey. How does it affect the mood of the drawing?

Draw this flower.

Tip: Perhaps sketch out the basic shape first, then gradually add more detail using blocks of colour. This is a complex shape, so look carefully at the negative shape around the plant to help simplify it.

299 ——————— Fill a page with drawings of water. You could use wax pastels to create vivid colours, and blend them with a brush and water if they are water-soluble.

300

Turn the splodges into animals.

301 ———— Draw things you love about summer.

302 ———— Draw something you really enjoyed about today.

303

Using your hands to make a viewfinder, draw an unusual and interesting composition below. Consider positioning your main subject off-centre, or even partially cropped outside of the composition.

Draw a zebra's stripes using pen and ink.

305 ———— Draw the materials in your pencil case.

306 ———— Create a pattern using abstract shapes and marks.

307 Continue drawing a line using a fine liner pen, then colour in the shapes using coloured pencils.

308 Use wax pastel to create lines of simple pattern.

309

Draw a face using torn or cut paper. You can be as detailed or abstract as you like.

Tip: You could draw onto the paper first using coloured pencils.

310

Colour each orange in a different style or material.

Draw a fireworks display.

Tip: Perhaps use wax pastels — you may want to protect the opposite page from smudges by adding a layer of tracing paper on top of this page.

312

Practise drawing the human figure by drawing on top of these sketches, or 'maquettes'. Flesh out the bodies. Add bulk to them, skin, hair and clothes.

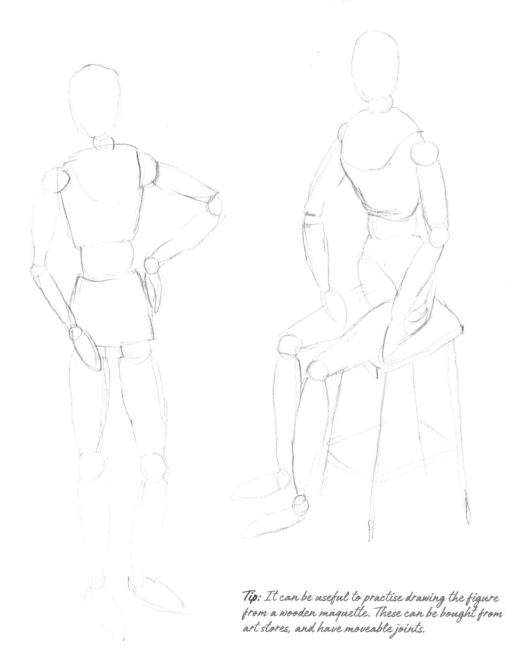

Tip: It can be useful to practise drawing the figure from a wooden maquette. These can be bought from art stores, and have moveable joints.

313 ———— Fill this page with drawings of eyes from life or photographs. Observe the different shapes and colours.

Draw your hand using only blue hues.

Tip: As well as creating a different mood to your drawing, using unnatural hues means that we concentrate on the tone and shape of the object, without being distracted by the colours. Try not to confuse hues of colour with tone, and squint your eyes to identify the areas of true shadow.

315 ——— Add colour to the starfish.

316 ——— Add elements to the tree, such as leaves and birds.

317

Draw a river from your imagination. Perhaps it is a cross-section showing the wildlife beneath the water, or an aerial view.

Complete a study of a flower using coloured pencils.

1. Carefully draw the outline. Press lightly, using a sharp coloured pencil.

2. Start to simplify the image you see, by adding the blocks of colour where you see them.

3. Add tone, from light to dark. Squinting your eyes as you look at the flower may help to see the light and dark tones.

4. Add detail with sharp coloured pencils. The final stage should be adding a small amount of the darkest tone you see, and highlights with white pencil.

319

Draw a face using just a few (8–10) lines. Perhaps you just suggest the edge of the face with one line, rather than drawing the whole face shape. The lines can be curved, straight or round, but try not to remove your pen from the page more than 10 or so times.

Tip: Sometimes it can be difficult to know when to stop with a drawing as it is finished. Allow yourself to keep this drawing simple, and stop after you've made the 10 lines. This may take some consideration and practise, but it's a great exercise to try if you feel like you overwork drawings.

—————

Practise sketching one person's face in lots of drawing studies below. Draw them from many different angles. Creating a few quick drawing studies are useful to do before you start a more sustained drawing of someone, as it helps you to really understand their face. The more you look at a face, the more you see, and the easier it will be to draw.

Tip: Perhaps choose a family member or friend as your subject. They may let you sketch them as you chat! You could also draw a news reader as they read the news on TV, or a presenter.

321

Draw skies below. Consider how the sky changes at different times of day. Perhaps note down the time next to each drawing.

Tones, from dark to light, can be created in lots of ways using watercolours. Use the boxes below to explore how the colour goes from dark to light as you move across the page.

Create thick downwards strokes by applying pressure to the brush. Once you've completed one stroke, lift the brush from the page and move from left to right.

Create thin downwards strokes by applying minimal pressure to the brush. Once you've completed one stroke, lift the brush from the page and move from left to right.

Using one long stroke, drag the brush from left to right.

Move the brush up and down in tight zig-zags from left to right, without lifting it from the page.

323 ——— Draw tropical leaves using watercolour. Perhaps the leaves overlap each other, to form an abstract print.

324 ——— Write a stream of conciousness. Just write what comes into your mind. There's no need to read it back.

325 ——————— Even when creating an observational drawing, your artwork doesn't need to be accurate and technically correct. Use the space below to create an expressive drawing.

Tip: It's still important to look at the subject of your drawing, but instead of measuring and looking at precise angles, make marks quickly and focus on the essence of what you see.

326 —————— Fill a page with circles of warm colours.

327 —————— Add layers of sand and soil,
and then plants, to the terrariums.

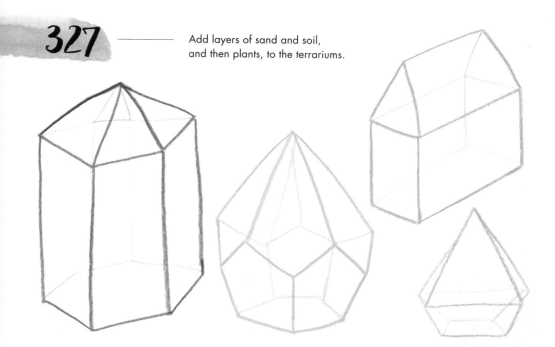

328 ———————— Fill this quarter page with purple dots.
Notice how many shades you can make.

329 ———————— Using the coloured background as your base, use light coloured wax pastels to draw. Perhaps draw a drinking glass, rain or a puddle, so that the blue can become part of your drawing.

Draw the fish.

331 ———— Fill the space with tiles of green. Notice how many different hues of green there are.

332 ———— Without using any written words, draw symbols to represent something that was memorable about your day today. Perhaps a sun for good weather, or a smiling face for good company.

333 ——————— Draw a landscape. This can be any location. Perhaps the horizon is very low and there is a lot of sky, or maybe the landscape is made from buildings. This could be a view from your home, or even a scene from a documentary.

Draw what is being illuminated by the light.

Fill the page with observational drawings of flowers.
You could try using a variety of different materials.

There are lots of ways you can draw the human body, and a good way to start is by blocking out the main bulk of the figure.

Using photographs of friends and family for reference, explore drawing the mass of the body using blocks of shape. You can use any material for this, perhaps try a range of different ones.

Once you have the hang of capturing the basic shape and position of the figures, you can then add detail and tone.

Tip: Consider the structure of the skeleton as you draw the body. It helps to keep in mind that an arm and leg can only bend naturally in certain places.

338 —————— Fill a page with cool shades of colours.

339 —————— Fill the page with doodles before you go to sleep.

340 —————— Draw something yellow.

341 —————— Add detail to the forest. Add leaves, texture, branches and birds.

342 ——— Fill the space with drawings of shoes. Use different colours and techniques.

343 ——— Draw a jungle.

344 — Add features to these faces using the axis as a guide. The eyes and ears are about halfway down the face. Notice where the halfway line is on each face and how this will effect the direction face is looking.

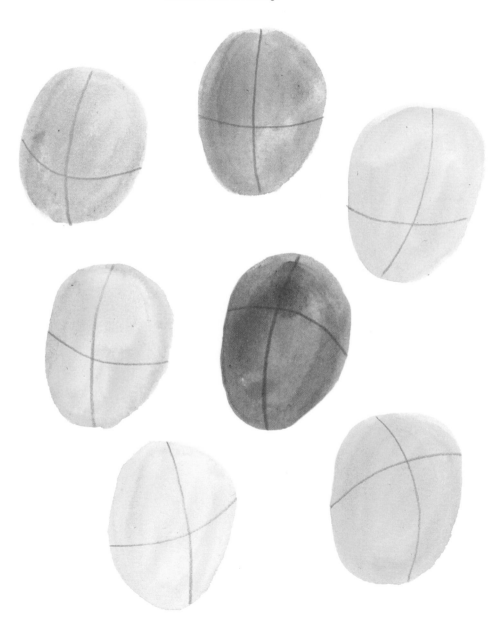

345 —————— Fill this page with drawings of mouths. Are they smiling? Are there teeth? Observe different colours and shapes.

Design a stack of bowls. Consider using pattern and choosing colours that work well together.

———————— Draw lilypads. Perhaps add water, frogs and flowers.

348 ———— Explore using a fine liner pen to create loops, small and large.

349 ———— Draw the profile of a face (the side view) using only the negative shape.

350

Fill each segment with different patterns, using 3–5 analogous colours. You may like to refer to your colour wheel for this task.

351 ———— Draw a meal or food that you enjoy.

352 ———— Draw a collection of clothing – tops, trousers, skirts.

353   —   Using your non-dominant hand (the opposite hand to the one you draw with) and without looking at reference, draw some people.

Tip: This could produce interesting results, as it will take you out of your comfort zone.

354   —   Fill this whole area with doodles.

Tip: Doodling is a great way to be creative, and helps to build confidence whilst drawing as there is no pressure to create anything in particular.

355 ———— Complete the shoal of fish.

356 ———— Continue drawing circles in any material.

357 — Add colours to create different palettes.

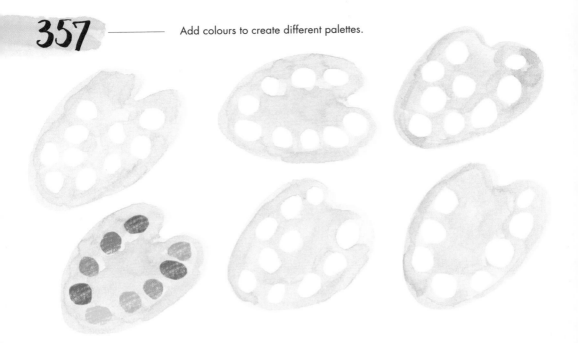

358 — Draw a scene around the river.

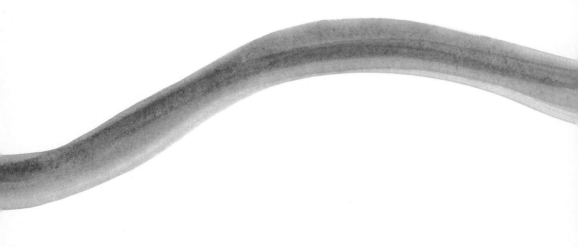

359 ——— Fill this quarter page with orange and yellow dots.

360 ——— Draw what you can see out of a window.

361

Try this sustained activity and use your **IMAGINATION** to create an image. Enjoy taking the time to let you mind wander.

ACTIVITY:

On the next pages, draw your favourite place in the world. This could be an imaginary travel destination, or somewhere closer to home. Close your eyes and think about that place. What colours can you see? What shapes or objects are there?

Is it a tropical island? A peaceful forest? Perhaps a city you've never visited?

Your drawing can be as abstract or as graphic as you like. Perhaps some areas are detailed, and others are left looser and more simplistic.

Use the page opposite to plan your drawing. Jot down ideas or key words – things you'd like to include in your image. Draw thumbnail sketches of possible compositions. You could also use the space to create swatches of your colour palette. Do the colours look good together? What mood do the colours create?

Then, using any materials you like, draw your scene on the next pages. You don't need to use the full space. Perhaps your drawing just shows a small window into a scene.

Tip: You could take inspiration from postcards, travel posters or old holiday snaps.

THINGS TO CONSIDER:

- There's no right or wrong answer with imaginitive drawing.

- Use this opportunity to think outside of the box and to be as creative as you can.

- If you are stuck for ideas, have a look back through the book, what did you enjoy drawing? Which colours did you get excited by?

Use this space to prepare for your drawing. Note down ideas, sketch thumbnails and create colour swatches of your palette.

362

Spend a period of time completing a drawing on the next page, using the skills you have practised in the **TUTORIAL** activities.

ACTIVITY:

Begin by choosing a subject to draw from life. Consider what you enjoy drawing, or perhaps set yourself a challenge by drawing something new that interests you. This could be a person, a still life, or a location. You could draw a face or whole body. You could even draw yourself whilst looking at your reflection.

Prepare for your drawing on the opposite page. Use your hands as a viewfinder to find a composition that appeals to you. Create some thumbnail sketches and plan out how your drawing will look. You could also use the space to create studies of the key features in your drawing – for example ears and eyes.

Once you are clear on what you will be drawing, turn over the page, and start your drawing by creating a rough sketch in pencil. Remember to check your angles and be sure the rough looks right. If not, don't be afraid to erase large areas and redraw. It's important to get the basic shapes and distances correct at this stage, so take as long as you need.

Tip: This is just a chance for you to explore what you've learnt, so enjoy the process rather than worrying about whether your drawing is good or bad.

THINGS TO CONSIDER:

- Be sure to really look, and draw what you see, rather than what you expect to see.

- Observe and measure angles and distances between shapes.

- If you decide to add tone to your drawing, build tone from light to dark, and squint to help identify the areas of shadow. Shadow and darker tones can be added in any colour, and it might be better to try to avoid using black as it can deaden your drawing.

- Observe the negative shape to help your mind simplify complex objects.

Warm up here with quick sketches of your subject and studies of key features.

You could create thumbnails of possible compositions here.

363

Spend some time completing this sustained **RELAXATION** activity. It may take you longer to complete than the previous exercises, but enjoy taking the time to just draw and create.

ACTIVITY:

Firstly, set aside a good chunk of time for yourself, so that you can draw without any time pressures and without interruption. Put on some calming music, or perhaps sit outside if you can.

Fill each circle on the next page with a pattern or design. Take your time on each design, so that you are being mindful of your decisions. Which colours will you choose? Which materials will you use?

You may like to try the warm up exercise on the opposite page first, to loosen your wrist and help wind down.

Tip: Remember to be in the moment. The focus of this task is not on the end result, but instead on enjoying the process of creation itself.

THINGS TO CONSIDER:

- These style activities can be used as a warm up at any time.

- Focusing your mind entirely on the task, choosing colours, thinking about pattern and enjoying being in the moment is a great way to bring mindfulness into your day.

- Drawing is a great way to distrsct your mind from everyday worries. If you feel like you need to give yourself a break, pick up a pen and just start doodling.

- Tasks that don't require too much thinking can be therapeutic and relaxing.

- At the end you will have created a beautiful piece of artwork which will be something to be proud of.

Tip: If you feel like creating your own mindful task once you've completed this book, why not paint your own circles, and fill them with pattern.

Before starting the activity on the next page, complete this warm-up exercise.
Practise drawing curved lines. Feel the rhythm of the repetitive drawing.

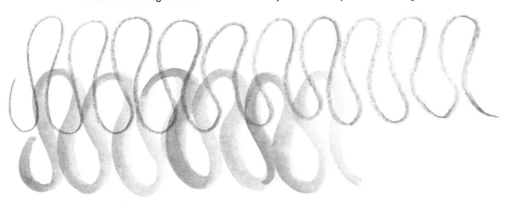

Take some time to explore **COLOUR THEORY** in this sustained activity. You may like to take this exploration further, outside of the pages of this book.

ACTIVITY:

Create a complementary palette. Choose two complementary colours, which are found opposite each other in the colour wheel. Using the steps on the opposite page, create a palette of colours using just these two these complementary colours and white.

Use paint for this, perhaps gouache, acrylic or watercolour. Mix these colours in a clean mixing palette, and swatch them on the next page.

Then, create a pattern using these colours. You can be sure the colours in your pattern will be harmonious if they all come from this palette you have created.

It could be a repeating pattern, or something more free and loose.

Use the darker colours in your palette to create tone, rather than being tempted to use black. You can also use white for highlight where needed.

Tip: You may like to refer back to your colour wheel for this exercise.

THINGS TO CONSIDER:

- It's useful to create a colour palette before you start a drawing. It makes decisions simpler when it comes to considering how you will add tone, as you can clearly see the darkest and lightest hues.

- You can create palettes just by eye, or perhaps by using 3–5 analogous colours.

- When creating a colour palette for future drawings, consider using less saturated hues alongside the bright ones. Add white to create less saturated colours, such as the hues you will create on the next page.

1. To create your complementary palette, start by swatching your two complementary colours each side of the paint palette, and also on the page or separate piece of paper.

2. Then, mix the two colours together, creating swatches as you go, to create a complementary scale across the top of your page.

3. For the second row of swatches, mix a little bit of white into each tone.

4. Continue to add white to all your swatches so that with each row your hues get less saturated.

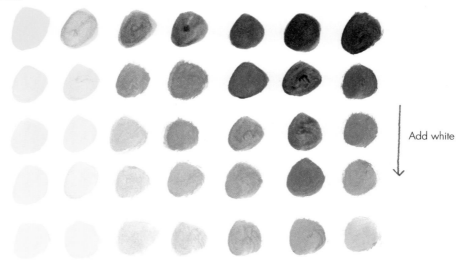

Add white

365

Complete a sustained **OBSERVATIONAL** drawing, by carefully studying something from life.

ACTIVITY:

Set up a still life scene in front of you. This could be a vase of flowers and fruit, or something less traditional. Choose shapes and objects that interest you, and that you feel inspired by.

Use everything you've practised in this book to draw the scene in whichever way you most enjoy, using any material you like. Use the next pages to draw the scene. Perhaps draw the scene a number of times, so the end result is a number of drawings of the same objects, in different styles and materials.

Remember to look carefully at the scene. Observe the scene for a couple of minutes before you start drawing. Move your eye around the outside of the shape.

Complete a blind drawing of the scene before you start, to warm up, and also so that you can focus on what you can see in front of you.

Tip: Drawings don't need to have outlines. You could draw your scene using blocks of colour and gradually build up the level of detail.

THINGS TO CONSIDER:

- You may like to complete a quick sketch before you start adding the details.

- Consider the palette you may like to use. How do the colours affect the mood of the drawing?

- Perhaps do some fast warm-up sketches of the scene, to get an idea of where everything belongs on the paper.

- Observe the negative shapes around the outside of the objects, and use this to help you draw accurate shapes.

- Build up your tone from light to dark. Swatch your tones before you start.

Complete a blind drawing of the scene. Draw what you see, without looking at the page. You could use a number of different colours to help identify various objects in the drawing.

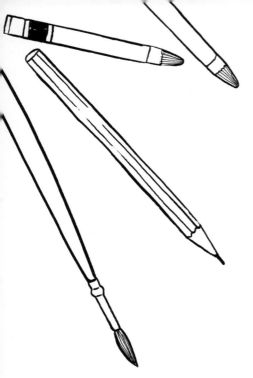

About the Author

Lorna Scobie grew up in the depths of the English countryside, climbing trees and taking her rabbit for walks in the fields. She is an illustrator and designer, now based in south London. Growing up surrounded by nature has heavily influenced her illustrations and her work often revolves around the natural world and the animal kingdom.

Lorna draws every day, and always has a sketchbook close to hand when she's out and about, just in case. She illustrates her work by hand rather than digitally, as she enjoys the spontaneity and also the 'happy mistakes' that can happen along the way. Her favourite places to draw are museums and botanical gardens.

If you'd like to keep up to date with Lorna's work, she can be found on Instagram and Twitter: **@lornascobie**

Thank you

To Joseph, Steven, Mum, Jill and Emma for their tips and ideas. Thank you also to my super editor, Kajal.

Published in 2018 by Hardie Grant Books, an imprint of Hardie Grant Publishing

Hardie Grant Books (London)
5th & 6th Floors
52–54 Southwark Street
London SE1 1UN

Hardie Grant Books (Melbourne)
Building 1, 658 Church Street
Richmond, Victoria 3121

hardiegrantbooks.com

British Library Cataloguing-in-Publication Data. A catalogue record for this book is available from the British Library.

365 Days of Drawing

ISBN: 978-1-78488-195-5

10 9

FSC
www.fsc.org
MIX
Paper from
responsible sources
FSC® C020056

Publisher: Kate Pollard
Commissioning Editor: Kajal Mistry
Illustrations: Lorna Scobie

Colour Reproduction by p2d
Printed and bound in China by Leo Paper Productions Ltd.